Can't You Guys Read?

S. harris

RUTGERS UNIVERSITY PRESS
New Brunswick, New Jersey

CAN'T YOU GUYS READ?

Cartoons on Academia
Sidney Harris

All the cartoons in this book have been previously published and copyrighted by the following periodicals: *Clinical Chemistry News, Changing Times, Chicago Magazine, The Chronicle of Higher Education, Datamation, Johns Hopkins Magazine, Phi Delta Kappan, National Law Journal, Playboy, Punch, Science, Wall Street Journal, Washingtonian,* and some extinct magazines, including the late, lamented *Saturday Review.* The cartoons have been reprinted with permission, and our thanks go to all the above publications.

The following cartoons are copyrighted by and reprinted with the permission of *The New Yorker* Magazine, Inc.: page 16 (1982), page 32 (1985), page 63 (1990), page 103 (1979), page 107 (1983), page 109 (1982).

Library of Congress Cataloging-in-Publication Data

Harris, Sidney.
    Can't you guys read? cartoons on academia / Sidney Harris.
      p.   cm.
    ISBN 0-8135-1733-8 (pbk.)
    1. Education—Caricatures and cartoons.   2. American wit and humor, Pictorial.   I. Title.
    NC1429.H33315A4 1991a
    741.5'973—dc20   91-12314
                                              CIP

British Cataloging-in-Publication information available

Manufactured in the United States of America.

FOR GLORIA AND HAROLD

Can't You Guys Read?

"THE UNIVERSITY IS NAMING A CHAIR FOR ME — IN THE LOUNGE."

2

"OH, DEAR! ANOTHER TRAGIC CASE OF MATH ANXIETY!"

5

BUSINESS GOTHIC
It was a dark and stormy night. From the heavy, brooding clouds poured great torrents of rain, a cold rain, whipped to a frenzy by a biting, metallic wind.
"If this keeps up," he thought, " I should be able to sell at least two dozen umbrellas an hour..."
S. Harris

"HI, I WORK AT THE ADMISSIONS OFFICE OF THE LOCAL UNIVERSITY. IF YOU COULD CHANGE THE WORLD IN THREE DAYS, WHAT WOULD YOU DO?"

"'C' IN ASTROPHYSICS, 'B MINUS' IN CALCULUS...
WHAT KIND OF GENIUS ARE YOU?"

"READ ANY GREAT BOOKS OF THE WESTERN WORLD LATELY?"

TYPE A FRESHMAN
CHANGED COURSES FOUR TIMES, GOT A JOB, ORGANIZED A PROTEST, QUIT THE JOB, PLANS TO TAKE SECOND SEMESTER ABROAD

"Dictionary."

As Lucanus, a giant bug, awoke one morning from uneasy dreams, he found himself transformed into Franz Kafka.

"MY BELIEF IS IF YOU'RE OLD ENOUGH TO TAKE 'TEXTS, COUNTER-TEXTS AND META-TEXTS IN WESTERN PHILOSOPHY', YOU SHOULD BE OLD ENOUGH TO DRINK."

"It's Dostoevsky. It's Melville. It's Flaubert. But it doesn't dance."

"AS IF THE PAPER SHORTAGE ISN'T BAD ENOUGH, NOW I HEAR THERE'S AN INK SHORTAGE."

"HE MAY HAVE A PH.D. IN ELEMENTARY PARTICLE PHYSICS, BUT HE'S HAVING AN AWFUL LOT OF TROUBLE WITH THE APPLICATION FORM."

THE MILBROOK VERNEY CHAIR IN LITERATURE

THE C.K. FREBISH ENDOWMENT FOR FOOTNOTES

"THERE ARE ESSENTIALLY FOUR BASIC FORMS FOR A JOKE — THE CONCEALING OF KNOWLEDGE LATER REVEALED, THE SUBSTITUTION OF ONE CONCEPT FOR ANOTHER, AN UNEXPECTED CONCLUSION TO A LOGICAL PROGRESSION AND SLIPPING ON A BANANA PEEL."

LINCOLN STANDARDIZED TEST CENTER
FORMERLY
LINCOLN HIGH SCHOOL

S. Harris

"I STICK WITH THE CELEBRITY INSTRUCTORS. IF I HEARD OF THEM, I SIGN UP WITH THEM."

LESSONS FROM THE BLAKELY ART SCHOOL (NOW DEFUNCT)

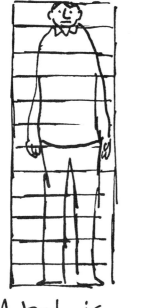

A body is
12 heads high

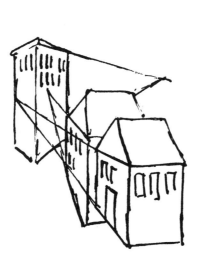

Every object has its
own vanishing point

Light comes from
many sources

"CONGRATULATIONS, AND THANKS FOR THE $86,000...
CONGRATULATIONS, AND THANKS FOR THE $86,000..."

"SINCE YOU CONDUCT ONLY THOUGHT-EXPERIMENTS, WE WERE HOPING YOU WOULD, FROM TIME TO TIME, COME UP WITH SOME THOUGHT-RESULTS."

"YOU SAY YOU'LL COME BACK, BUT NO ONE EVER RETURNS TO THIS NEIGHBORHOOD AFTER GRADUATION FROM AGRICULTURAL SCHOOL."

BULLETIN BOARD
Ms Flanders loves teaching.
If any students love learning, apply to room 349.
MEETING
S. Harris

"SINCE GREG WAS ACCEPTED BY MENSA, HE'D RATHER NOT SAY ANYTHING THAN SAY SOMETHING INCORRECT."

"CAN'T YOU GUYS READ?"

"5/3 OF THE CLASS DON'T UNDERSTAND A WORD I'M SAYING ABOUT FRACTIONS."

INFLUENCES

"THAT'S RODERICK SLOAN, THE ALVIN MERIWETHER PROFESSOR OF BUSINESS ADMINISTRATION, AND WITH HIM IS ALVIN MERIWETHER, THE RODERICK SLOAN PROFESSOR OF ECONOMICS."

"I HEARD IT'S A DIPLOMA MILL."

RAPID READING CENTER
HERGESHEIMER, BATTENKORN, DONIZETELLO, KATELLENDORF, McILHENESSEY, RUDEMACHER, & SZYMANSKOWICZ
ATTORNEYS AT LAW
Hergesheimer, Battenkorn, Donizetello, Katellendorf, McIlhenessey, Rudemacher, & Szymanskowicz
Attorneys at Law
S. Harris

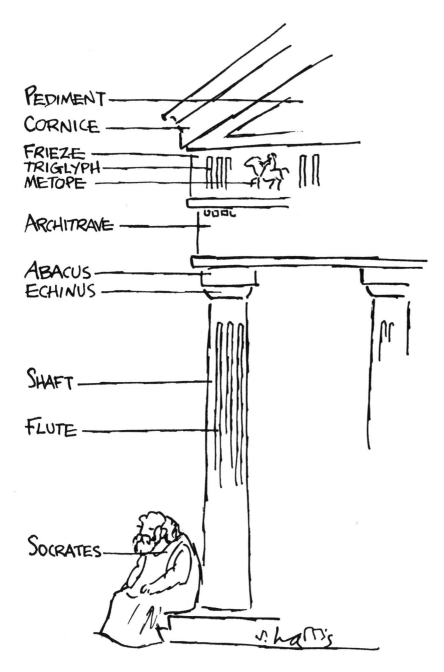

PEDIMENT

CORNICE

FRIEZE
TRIGLYPH
METOPE

ARCHITRAVE

ABACUS
ECHINUS

SHAFT

FLUTE

SOCRATES

MAKING PHILOSOPHY ACCESSIBLE: POP-UP PLATO

"ARE YOU SURE
EINSTEIN STARTED THIS WAY?"

LEOPARD FROG
(Rana Pipiens)

IN HONOR OF THOSE WHO
MET THEIR FATE AT THE
HANDS OF AN UNTOLD NUMBER
OF BIOLOGY STUDENTS

"ABOUT THE CURRICULUM: 'THE CONTEMPORARY NOVEL FROM AUSTEN TO DICKENS'..."

"I DON'T HAVE THE TEST I SCHEDULED FOR TODAY. MY DOG ATE IT."

"HERE WE ARE, LIVING THE GREAT AMERICAN NOVEL, AND THERE'S NO ONE TO WRITE IT DOWN FOR US."

"IF HIS I.Q. IS BASED ON GUESSING THE RIGHT ANSWERS, PERHAPS WE COULD ASSUME HE'LL GO THROUGH LIFE BEING A REMARKABLY SUCCESSFUL GUESSER."

"IT TURNS OUT NOBODY HAS ANYTHING TO SAY."

IN WRITING WAR AND PEACE, TOLSTOY WAS GOING FOR THE BIG LAUGH, BUT THE MORE HE WROTE, THE MORE ELUSIVE IT BECAME.

"GRIDLY, TRY NOT TO TELL TOO MANY PEOPLE THAT YOU WENT TO THIS SCHOOL."

"HE DISCOVERED HE'S NOT IN THE PROPAEDIA, HE'S NOT IN THE MICROPAEDIA AND HE'S NOT IN THE MACROPAEDIA."

"GOT IDEA. TALK BETTER. COMBINE WORDS. MAKE SENTENCES."

"WELL, MR. THOREAU, WE'RE INTERESTED IN PUBLISHING YOUR VIEWS ON GOVERNMENT AUTHORITY AND PERSONAL FREEDOM, BUT PERHAPS YOU COULD LEAVE OUT SOME OF THE REFERENCES TO LIMA BEANS AND TURNIPS."

"THE ADDITION IS EASY — BUT I TEND TO BE NONVERBAL, AND THE APPLES THROW ME."

"WHAT WE ESPECIALLY LIKE ABOUT THESE THEORETICAL TYPES IS THAT THEY DON'T TIE UP THOUSANDS OF DOLLARS WORTH OF EQUIPMENT."

GALILEO'S BURDEN

I WAS ALWAYS QUITE A DISAPPOINTMENT TO MY PARENTS. THEY WANTED ME TO BECOME A DOCTOR.

"REMEMBER, ALL THESE LIFE EXPERIENCES CAN SOMEDAY BE USED AS COLLEGE CREDIT."

"BIG DEAL — A GUY WRITES A COUPLE OF PLAYS, AND SUDDENLY HE THINKS HE'S THE SPOKESMAN FOR HIS GENERATION."

"AT LEAST IT DOESN'T APPEAR TO BE A CASE OF <u>SENSELESS</u> VIOLENCE."

"WHAT'S THE BIG SURPRISE? ALL THE LATEST THEORIES OF LINGUISTICS SAY WE'RE BORN WITH THE INNATE CAPACITY FOR GENERATING SENTENCES."

"You're everyman? I thought I was everyman."

INTERDISCIPLINARY STUDIES

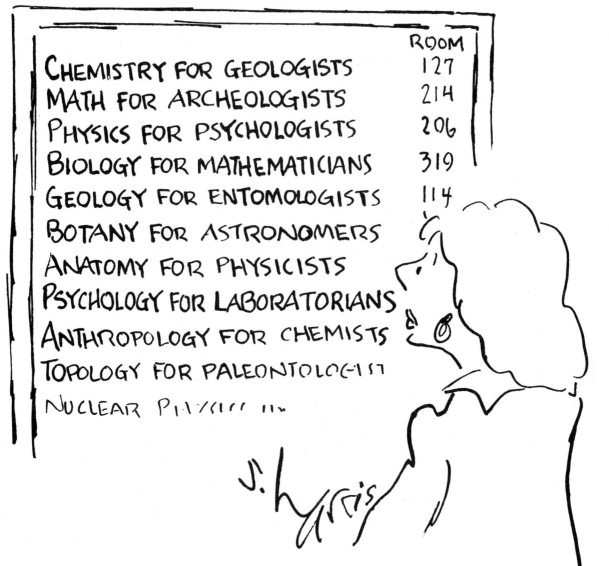

	ROOM
CHEMISTRY FOR GEOLOGISTS	127
MATH FOR ARCHEOLOGISTS	214
PHYSICS FOR PSYCHOLOGISTS	206
BIOLOGY FOR MATHEMATICIANS	319
GEOLOGY FOR ENTOMOLOGISTS	114
BOTANY FOR ASTRONOMERS	
ANATOMY FOR PHYSICISTS	
PSYCHOLOGY FOR LABORATORIANS	
ANTHROPOLOGY FOR CHEMISTS	
TOPOLOGY FOR PALEONTOLOGIST	
NUCLEAR PHYSICS	

"I WILL NOW ANNOUNCE THE NAMES OF THE GRADUATES, IN THE ORDER OF THE STARTING SALARIES OFFERED TO THEM."

"COMPULSORY EDUCATION IS A MYTH. WE MAY BE COMPELLED TO TEACH, BUT VERY FEW OF THEM ARE COMPELLED TO LEARN."

"DON'T YOU SEE, KREUTZER? THAT'S WHY WE HAVE ALL THIS LITERATURE. SO YOU WON'T DUPLICATE AN EXPERIMENT THAT'S ALREADY BEEN DONE. AND THERE'S NO REASON AT ALL WHY YOU SHOULD BE DUPLICATING SMEDLY'S EXPERIMENTS. AFTER ALL, HE SHARES A LAB WITH YOU."

SAMUEL COLERIDGE TRYING TO ESTABLISH THE LOCATION OF THE ALBATROSS

S. Harris

"MICKLEBAR KNEW MORE ABOUT SOMETHING THAN ANYONE ELSE, BUT HE'S FORGOTTEN WHAT IT IS."

"WE REALIZE YOU DO BETTER ON YOUR I.Q. TESTS THAN YOU DO IN ANYTHING ELSE, BUT YOU JUST CANNOT MAJOR IN I.Q."

"EACH ONE REPRESENTS ANOTHER HONOR."

"ONE THING I'LL ALWAYS BE THANKFUL FOR IS THAT I GOT HERE BEFORE THERE <u>WERE</u> ANY SATs."

1.

2.

1. Prozorov, Andrey Serghyeevich
2. Natasha (Natalia Ivanovna)
3. Olga (Olga Serghyeevna, Olia)
4. Masha (Maria Serghyeevna)
5. Irena (Irena Serghyeevna)
6. Koolyghin, Fiodor Ilyich
7. Vershinin, Alexandr Ignatyevich

"SURE THERE'S A WAY TO DISCIPLINE THEM. YELL AT THEM."

"YOU GOT INTO THE COLLEGE OF MY CHOICE, AND I GOT INTO THE COLLEGE OF YOUR CHOICE. NOW, IF WE COULD JUST WORK SOMETHING OUT..."

"FROM WHAT I HEAR, THE ATWOOD INTUITION TANK IS COMING UP WITH RESULTS FASTER THAN WE ARE."

"WHAT A LOUSY SEASON — THERE HASN'T BEEN A GOOD COMEDY IN MONTHS."

"YES, I AGREE THAT MAN IS MASTER OF HIS OWN DESTINY, BUT SOMETIMES IT HELPS IF YOU PASS ALGEBRA."

"GETTING AN 'A' OR A STAR IS ALL RIGHT, BUT I'D LIKE SOME SORT OF PROFIT-SHARING PLAN AROUND HERE."

HAVING FINISHED WRITING HIS LATEST 400-PAGE NOVEL, ANTON CHEKHOV DIVIDES IT INTO 32 SHORT STORIES

"THE WORD GOING AROUND IS THAT THE BUSINESS ADMINISTRATION GRADUATES ARE HIRING THE ENGINEERING GRADUATES."

figure 1.

figure 2.

figure 3.

figure 4.

S. Harris

CAN YOU BELIEVE HOW MANY STUDENTS CAN'T IDENTIFY SOCRATES, HEMINGWAY AND CHURCHILL?
WHO?
S. Harris

"I THINK HE KNOWS SOMETHING THAT WE DON'T KNOW ABOUT THE URANIUM MOLECULE."

"IF YOU WANT TO KNOW HOW STODGY THIS PLACE IS, TALK TO DR. FIRBANK, OUR FOOTBALL COACH."

"LOOK, TOM, LOOK. IT IS GOOD. YES. GOOD. THE END. PUBLISHED BY KALEIDOSCOPIC ENTERPRISES. 437 SCHERMERHORN BOULEVARD."

"DO WE NEED THIS EVEN IF WE'RE NOT PLANNING TO GO TO COLLEGE?"

"I'LL SAY THIS FOR YOUNG THOREAU — HE CERTAINLY DOES MAKE GOOD USE OF HIS POND."

COLLEGE
OF
ARTS & SCIENCES
(AND A FEW THINGS
TO FALL BACK ON)

"I TOLD THEM THAT REFUSING TO READ DICKENS IS LIKE REFUSING TO DO ALGEBRA. NOW THEY REFUSE TO DO ALGEBRA."

"IS THIS THE WAY YOU PLAN TO SPEND YOUR PEAK LEARNING YEARS?"

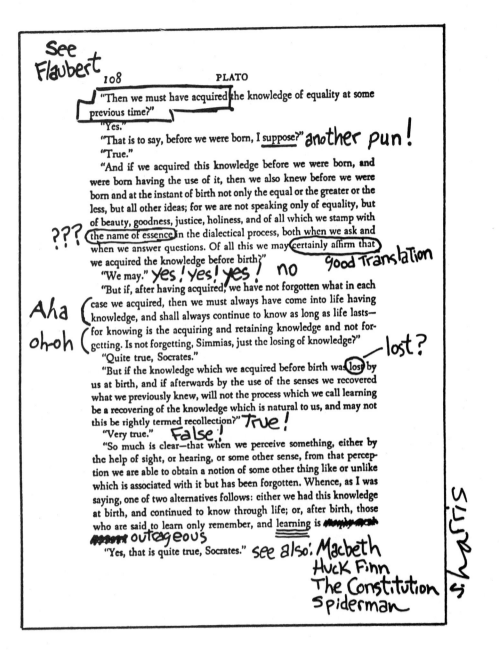

See Flaubert

"Then we must have acquired the knowledge of equality at some previous time?"

"Yes."

"That is to say, before we were born, I suppose?" *another pun!*

"True."

"And if we acquired this knowledge before we were born, and were born having the use of it, then we also knew before we were born and at the instant of birth not only the equal or the greater or the less, but all other ideas; for we are not speaking only of equality, but of beauty, goodness, justice, holiness, and of all which we stamp with the name of essence in the dialectical process, both when we ask and when we answer questions. Of all this we may certainly affirm that we acquired the knowledge before birth?" *???   no   good Translation*

"We may." *yes! yes! yes!*

"But if, after having acquired, we have not forgotten what in each case we acquired, then we must always have come into life having knowledge, and shall always continue to know as long as life lasts— for knowing is the acquiring and retaining knowledge and not forgetting. Is not forgetting, Simmias, just the losing of knowledge?" *Aha   oh-oh*

"Quite true, Socrates."

"But if the knowledge which we acquired before birth was lost by us at birth, and if afterwards by the use of the senses we recovered what we previously knew, will not the process which we call learning be a recovering of the knowledge which is natural to us, and may not this be rightly termed recollection?" *True!* *lost?*

"Very true." *False!*

"So much is clear—that when we perceive something, either by the help of sight, or hearing, or some other sense, from that perception we are able to obtain a notion of some other thing like or unlike which is associated with it but has been forgotten. Whence, as I was saying, one of two alternatives follows: either we had this knowledge at birth, and continued to know through life; or, after birth, those who are said to learn only remember, and learning is ~~simply a~~ ~~recollection~~ outrageous

"Yes, that is quite true, Socrates." *see also: Macbeth Huck Finn The Constitution Spiderman*

is harris

MEMORY SCHOOL

IMPROVE
RETENTION
CAPACITY
RECALL

IF AMNESIA
PERSISTS
SEE YOUR
PHYSICIAN

J. Harris

"HE'S A PRODIGY, ALL RIGHT, BUT ALL HIS WORK DEALS WITH SUBJECTS SUCH AS THE ELASTICITY OF BUBBLE GUM, THE DECIBEL LIMITS OF ROCK RECORDS AND THE MOLECULAR CONTENT OF A CHEESEBURGER."

"AFTER BEING HERE FOR MORE THAN FORTY YEARS — AS UNDERGRADUATE, GRADUATE STUDENT INSTRUCTOR, PROFESSOR — WHAT SADDENS ME MOST IS THAT THIS WAS NOT THE COLLEGE OF MY CHOICE."

WRITER'S BLOCK

Temporary

Permanent

"SAY, BABY—
'COME LIVE WITH ME AND BE MY LOVE,
AND WE WILL ALL THE PLEASURES PROVE,
THAT VALLEYS, GROVES, HILLS AND FIELDS,
WOODS OR STEEPY MOUNTAIN YIELDS.'
MARLOWE."

FAILED ALLIANCE

"YOU SIMPLY ASSOCIATE EACH NUMBER WITH A WORD, SUCH AS 'TABLE' AND 3,476,029."

"THIS IS GETTING TO BE TOO MUCH FOR ME. I'M THINKING OF BECOMING A MIDDLEBROW."

THE GLOBE
PLAYHOUSE

'HAMLET'
A NEW PLAY BY
Wᴹ SHAKESPEARE
"YOU'LL COME OUT
QUOTING"

S. harris

"THIS IS DR. GRUMBACHER, PROFESSOR EMERITUS OF COMPARATIVE PHILOLOGY. PERHAPS HE COULD TELL YOU THE DIFFERENCE BETWEEN AN ADVERB AND AN ADJECTIVE."

"IT'S SOME INTELLECTUAL GROUP, BUT
NOBODY CAN FIGURE OUT WHAT THEY WANT."

"TRIAL AND ERROR — THAT'S WHAT I MISS."

"I'VE GOTTEN QUITE A BIT OUT OF THAT CREATIVE WRITING CLASS. I THINK I'LL BECOME A LITERARY AGENT."

"IT'S UP TO YOU, MR. SNEDLY. GET IT FIXED, OR ENTER IT IN THE ANTIQUE SHOW."

About The Author: This caption was written by Marty Read of Louisville, Ky. Mr. Read has written seven other captions, including, "Hi ya, hubby! Good 7,213th morning of our wedded bliss to you.", and The famous "All we own can be tumble-dried."

"WHAT YOU'VE DONE, MR. HATTEN, IS YOU'VE CROSSED THAT THIN LINE BETWEEN FINE LITERATURE AND ANNUAL REPORT."

WASN'T IT KIERKEGAARD WHO SAID 'WE PERCEIVE LIFE THROUGH THE FILTER OF OUR LIVES, AND THOUGH THE WORLD REMAINS VIRTUALLY UNCHANGED, WE SEE IT CHANGING CONTINUALLY'?
NO, KIERKEGAARD NEVER SAID ANYTHING LIKE THAT.
S. HARRIS

"I MAJORED IN ETHICS. SEVERAL RECRUITERS TALKED TO ME. THEY'D LIKE ME TO DO VOLUNTEER WORK."

"AS I SEE IT, PINOCCHIO WAS MOTIVATED BY A NEED TO PROVE HIMSELF, WHILE BOTH HANSEL AND GRETEL WERE DRIVEN BY AN INBORN REBELLIOUSNESS."

"THERE'S BEEN A SLIGHT MISTAKE. 1542 WASN'T THE AVERAGE SAT SCORE—IT WAS THE NUMBER OF STUDENTS WHO TOOK THE TEST."

"...AND THE RECRUITER FROM IBM — DID YOU ALSO TELL HIM THAT AT COLLEGE YOU MOSTLY SAT ON A ROCK BY THE SEA, TRYING TO FIND YOURSELF?"

"NEVER MIND INSPIRATION. I NEED BACKGROUND MATERIAL ON ATOMIC PHYSICS."

"LET'S GET DOWN TO BASICS. WHAT'S THE OUTLOOK FOR THINK TANKS IN THE NEXT CENTURY?"

'STRUTS' LEBOW, BATTING .347, RECEIVES $4,200 GRANT IN HITTING TO SUPPLEMENT HIS $1,630,000 SALARY

SLOW
READING
INSTITUTE

Learn to
Enjoy
ADJECTIVES
METAPHORS
ALLITERATION
Again

"ACTUALLY THIS IS A VERY EXPERIMENTAL COLLEGE. WE HAVE NO CURRICULUM AND NO CLASSES. HOW IT WORKS, ESSENTIALLY, IS IF YOU WANT TO LEARN SOMETHING, YOU GO SOMEPLACE AND YOU LEARN IT."

"MY INVENTION IS EVEN MORE REMARKABLE THAN YOURS. IT IS THE SIMPLE DECLARATIVE SENTENCE."

"...AND, AS YOU GO OUT INTO THE WORLD, I PREDICT THAT YOU WILL, GRADUALLY AND IMPERCEPTIBLY, FORGET ALL YOU EVER LEARNED AT THIS UNIVERSITY."